Rocky
Life as a Guide Dog Puppy

Written by Margot Bennett

with help from Rocky

Copyright © 2023 by Margot Bennett.

All rights reserved worldwide. No part of this publication may be reproduced, distributed or transmitted in any form or by any means, including photocopying, recording, or other electronic or mechanical methods, without the prior written permission of the publisher, except in the case of brief quotations embodied in critical reviews and certain other noncommercial uses permitted by copyright law. Please do not participate in or encourage piracy of copyrighted materials in violation of the author's rights. Purchase only authorized editions.

For permission requests, email tailsofdogswhohelp@gmail.com

Story and photography by Margot Bennett
Cover design by flamescreations
Photo modifications created using Photo Lab
Chapter 1 photography by Guiding Eyes for the Blind
Book design by Sarah E. Holroyd (https://sleepingcatbooks.com)

Rocky, Life as a Guide Dog Puppy/Margot Bennett — 1st ed.
Published
LCCN: 2023908296
Hardcover ISBN: 978-1-7357990-6-3
Paperback ISBN: 978-1-7357990-7-0
Ebook ISBN: 978-1-7357990-8-7

Produced in the United States of America

This book is dedicated to all those involved in the journey to becoming a guide dog–the staff and volunteers at the Canine Development Center and Guiding Eyes for the Blind® in New York, puppy raisers, donors, administrative staff and of course, the graduates. Graduates are provided guide dogs at no cost thanks to all those involved in the puppy raising experience. Guiding Eyes puppies are loved and cared for from before their birth until they have passed over the rainbow bridge.

I hope you enjoy the journey of one of these amazing dogs, Rocky.

Proceeds from *Rocky, Life as a Guide Dog Puppy* are donated to Guiding Eyes to assist in providing training for present and future guide dogs.

Other books by Margot Bennett

Tails Of Dogs Who Help Series
Brisco, Life as a Therapy Dog, Book 1
Ely, Life as a Service Dog Puppy, Book 2

Introduction

Hello! My name is Rocky and I'm a yellow Labrador Retriever. I am a guide dog to a woman named Connie who is visually impaired. This means she cannot see like other people do. My job is to help her get around safely.

Guide dogs help assist their partners with independence. As a team, we keep each other safe as we work together!

Some ways I help:

- Crossing busy streets
- Stopping at stairs
- Turning left and right

Even though dogs don't do things like drive cars, cook food, or go to work, I can still be her eyes as she navigates the world—as long as she shows me the way.

Connie always gets me a yummy dog treat on our way home. *Mmmm...I am drooling just thinking about it.*

It wasn't easy though. It took a lot of time and training before I was able to do all this with Connie.

Come along and I will tell you my story!

Chapter 1
The "R" Litter is Born

My puppy sisters and I began our lives at the first-class Canine Development Center, where all puppies for *Guiding Eyes for the Blind*® are born. *Guiding Eyes* is a special organization that helps puppies train and become guide dogs like me!

When my sisters and I were born, we became the "R" litter. All of us would have names beginning with the letter "R."

I was the second puppy born that late summer night, weighing 1 pound 2 ounces. That is about the size of a jar of peanut butter!

Mmm, peanut butter.

I remember all the squeaks and squeals as we settled into the warmth and comfort of this new, human world. Other puppies were settling into this new place too.

Our days were filled with long naps. I loved to sleep in a small, puppy pile with my sisters—especially on top of the soft blankets that the humans carefully arranged for us.

During those first few weeks, we could not see or hear very well. We constantly bumped into each other as we squealed and crawled on our bellies across the playpen.

Garbo, our dog-mom, helped keep us safe and warm. She was a superstar mom to guide dogs all over the country!

Our tiny bodies began to grow. Our fur got soft and fuzzy. We were so little we slept a lot.

What is your favorite place to cuddle or nap?

Exploring New Things

In case you forgot, it is hard learning to walk. I remember tripping over my huge paws. Slowly my eyes adjusted and I began to see all the exciting things around me. Within days, my sisters and I were strong enough to romp inside the puppy playpen.

One day as I was chasing my sister, Rosa, I felt warm hands lift me. Someone carried me to a room filled with toys. My tummy fluttered a little. I was nervous.

What am I supposed to do with these strange things?

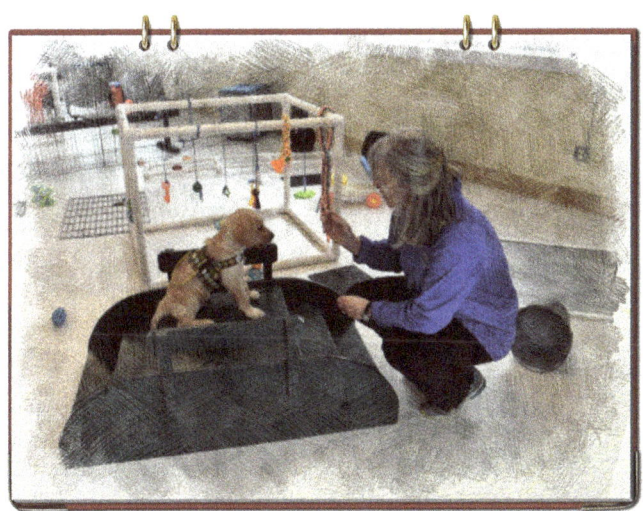

- Plastic slide—That's a long way down from the top!
- Wide open tunnels—I imagined a mouth wide open, waiting to eat me!
- Stairs to climb—I think I'm too tiny for even that first step!

Someone placed me in front of the tunnel and I stared into its dark, open mouth. I gathered my courage. Taking

a deep breath, I sprinted forward through the darkness, and came out on the other side. As I skidded to a stop, I almost ran into….*is that ME?!*

I peeked at what was peering back at me inside the frame. *Whoa! Who is that?* The puppy staring back at me seemed timid and curious. I sniffed at it, and it sniffed back. I turned my head right, and it turned its head left. *Hmm.* I glanced back as I trotted off to play elsewhere and the puppy had disappeared. *Will I see him again?*

I padded my way over lumps and bumps under my paws.

"You can do this!" a person cheered.

"Don't stop now! You can do it!" said someone behind me. I crept towards the slippery edge of the slide.

"You're learning!" Someone else encouraged me as I teetered onto the second bumpy step on the stairs.

As my sisters and I enjoyed our daily play routine, we were learning things to help us with our future roles as guide dogs. We just didn't know it yet.

Venturing Outside

Some days my sisters and I would follow humans to new places. Their encouraging voices kept us eager to tag along and discover where they were leading us. The first time we walked outside, my eyes squinted at the bright sunshine.

Each time the humans placed me on the lawn I lifted each of my paws hesitantly. *Ouch! That's pokey. But, it tickles, too!* After a few tries, I was able to put all four paws down at the same time. *Maybe the grass wasn't so bad after all.* I started running. *I was free!*

Suddenly, as I zoomed around the yard, a long bushy tail scurried past me. *Whoa! What was that?* I followed the tail until it scurried up the side of a tall tree. I needed to investigate this mysterious creature.

As I peered up the tree trunk trying to spot the bushy tail again, happy voices called to me from across the yard. I knew I needed to turn around and go back. But, that tail…I had to make a choice!

I will look for that mysterious creature another time.

I breathed in the fresh air as I playfully bounded back to the human. The inviting sights and smells would have to wait until tomorrow. Her smiling face and yummy kibble always won me over.

Kibble used for training is from the puppy's regular meal.

Spa Days

Every day the humans groomed and made a big fuss over us.

- Tiny baby clippers cut our soft toenails.
- Soft bristles brushed our fur.
- Fingers gently rubbed our ears.

I heard something and my ears perked up. Hearing new sounds, especially loud ones, could be scary, but it wasn't so bad when I was cradled in warm, human arms. Construction noises, piano music, and phones ringing echoed in the background as I fell asleep.

Lots of different sounds are played throughout the day...

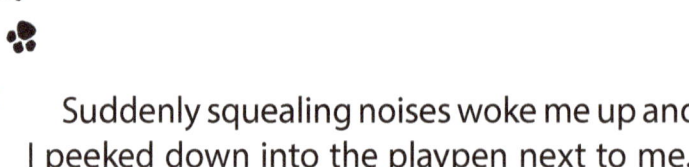

Suddenly squealing noises woke me up and I stretched. I peeked down into the playpen next to me. *Oh…yellow puppies just like me!! They must be new*! I wriggled and whined. I really wanted to hop into that puppy pile. *What letter of the alphabet do these puppies belong to?*

My human hugged me tightly. She wouldn't let me down there to play with them.

"Shh, Rocky. They're too little for you to play with right now."

I sighed, feeling sad. I just wanted to play with them. She lowered me gently back onto our bedding. Soon I fell asleep, dreaming of those tiny puppies frolicking all around me.

Weekend Field Trips

Soon we were six weeks old and as big as THREE jars of peanut butter! We began taking trips to a volunteer family for the weekend. I heard humans say this was an important role in our learning too.

These weekend trips introduced us to what it was like to live in a home. Staying in these homes brought new, but sometimes scary, experiences. The humans in this house were always busy—and they were always making noise!

- Roaring of the vacuum cleaner! The floor underneath me rumbled.
- Sloshing water for a child's bath! I dreamed of sloshing in my water dish.
- Chimes of the doorbells ringing! My ears echoed too.

After a while, these new sounds didn't bother me at all. There were things I loved about weekend visits—new smells. Cooking smells! Kid smells! Laundry smells! Some smelled delicious. Some did not.

Once the smell of something yummy on the floor caught my attention, and I couldn't resist. Just as I tried to snatch it and sneak a taste, I was scooped up by a grown-up.

"Silly Rocky," I heard as she hugged me. "That Cheerio is not for you."

After tossing the Cheerio into the garbage, she gently laid me down. A little human crawled up to me and

placed her head next to mine. We were both tired. Or maybe we were both disappointed there were no more Cheerios. Together, we fell asleep.

Our weekend trips were filled with playtime, sounds, food, and snuggles. The humans said that these were all important tools to help us become confident and successful guide dogs.

I was so happy to be learning all these exciting things, even though I wasn't sure what a guide dog was… yet.

Why is it important for a guide dog to not eat something off the floor?

Chapter 2
Journey to My Puppy Raiser

In no time at all, my sisters and I were eight weeks old. Excitement was in the air. I could feel the breeze as people rushed past me. I was picked up and placed on a cold, metal square. "19.6 pounds!" Every few minutes my ears caught phrases like "Are the kennels ready? Did you add lots of towels?" "Food zipped up tight?"

My sisters and I wagged our tails with excitement at the sound of all the kibble being poured out of the bag. This is going to be an extra-long trip...*or a really big meal!*

Phone calls were made to the puppy raisers to announce we were ready. What I didn't know at the time was how hard my own puppy raiser had worked to prepare for my arrival. Toys! Food! Bowl! Leash! Special bed and more! Puppies need a lot of stuff!

It was time for the next phase of my training.

I saw myself reflected in the mirror again and leaned my head to the left, watching as my mirror image leaned to the right. This puppy was bigger than the one I saw weeks ago. It stood up a bit straighter.

My tail swished back and forth, but my tummy was sending me a different message. *Would I still have fun learning with my puppy raiser?*

I took a deep breath and began to walk away, noticing a poster of a puppy who looked just like me. That puppy looked confident and curious.

Maybe I could be that too.

I can do this. I am going to make a difference to someone. Someday.

But how?

My Long Road Trip

My sisters and I were given lots of hugs and kisses—even more than usual! One by one, we were tucked into a kennel for our trip—Rosa in one car, Roxy and I in another. Roxy and I whispered excitedly. Each of us kept guessing where the other was going. As the hours passed, smells drifted in through the windows. I smelled food being grilled—*Yum!* There were cow smells from the field—*Not yum!* I tried to hold my breath until that smell went by. The smell of pine needles—*not sure!*

Every once and a while the car stopped, and we were carried to a clean spot for a potty break.

Phew! This was taking forever. I had already taken way more than my usual amount of puppy naps. *There are only so many things I can chase in my dreams!*

Sunlight was replaced by darkness, and we still hadn't arrived yet. I could feel my tummy rumbling. I was so happy when we stopped and were given some puppy mush. We slurped it up in no time! Then, it was back into the kennel to continue our journey.

Finally, the car stopped for good. I opened my eyes to peek.

We were here!

Meeting My Puppy Raiser

A light flashed into our eyes through the car window. My tail swished at hearing squeals of delight as the back of the car opened. I was lifted into the light, but Roxy stayed behind in the kennel as the door was closed again.

Wait—wasn't she going with me? The arms holding me turned so I could see her through the window again. She was curled back into a ball, fast asleep. *Roxy must know she will meet her puppy raiser next.*

Confident she was being cared for, I swiveled back around and gazed at the face of my new puppy raiser. She was tall and smelled of soap. I nuzzled her neck as she carried me inside and gently lowered me down. My nose smushed into the rug, tail swishing slowly as I sniffed in circles. I began to run, enjoying this new freedom of movement. High-pitched voices sounded behind me and I stopped to turn around.

Little humans! I ran as fast as my puppy paws could carry me.

A grown-up should always be nearby when children are with a dog.

Oh…let me find out if they like to snuggle! I picked up the first toy I saw, and nestled myself right into the little human's lap, anticipating her tiny hands on my back.

She hardly noticed me. She was just interested in my leash.

Hmmm. Let's try the other little humans.

When I trotted over, they hugged me tight and gave me a plush toy to gnaw on. As their hands rubbed my fur back and forth, I peeked up to see my puppy raiser smiling at us.

"Welcome home, Rocky," she said.

That night, I was exhausted by the long trip and the energy of the three little humans. I plopped down in the first quiet spot I could find and fell asleep. Little did I know that it would become my favorite spot—right in the middle of where the grown-ups needed to cook.

Questions floated around in my puppy dreams.

Chapter 3
Learning My New Home

The sun peeking through the gate of my kennel woke me up. *Hmm… How did I get here?* I relaxed, remembering my new home. The kennel door creaked as it was swung open.

"Good morning, sweet boy," my puppy raiser whispered.

I stretched my little legs in front of me, and quickly felt the need to use the bathroom. Before I could think twice, my puppy raiser carried me outside and placed me on some fresh, wet grass.

"Get busy," she said.

Boy, was I ready!

Not two seconds after I was done, my puppy raiser squealed. "Yes!" she said as she fed me kibble after kibble. "Good boy!" *Wow! All this for just going to the bathroom?*

All day I repeated this new information to myself.

Do what is asked and earn a treat.
Follow instructions and be given some kibble.

I could get used to this kind of learning.

What could I do next to earn more kibble?

Meeting Someone Spectacular

I scampered back inside and came to a crashing halt when I smelled...DOG! I closed my eyes for a second.
Was I dreaming?

Did you know that dogs can smell 1,000 to 10,000 times better than people?

When I opened my eyes, there was a large dog who looked just like me.

"Pssst," he whispered to me.

Me?

"I'm Decker, your new big brother. I'm going to help teach you the ropes.

"I am also going to be your friend and help teach you all things dog."

What is that round yellow thing in Decker's mouth?

"Ah." Decker sighed at me with a dog huff.
Wait? Did he just talk to me? He must speak dog!
"This is a tennis ball, the greatest invention ever for pet dogs. But I am not supposed to have it inside. Shh... Don't tell."

Decker jumped up and walked to the door, turning his head for me to follow. I followed him. Then, we waited for my puppy raiser.

Exploring the Yard

I had to remain at the open door until my puppy raiser released me. When I stepped outside, there were large trees and a gigantic area to just…run! Hold on, though. To get down to the yard, something was blocking my way.

STAIRS.

I had never seen stairs this BIG. I tucked my tail a bit and tiptoed to the edge, sniffing the scary barricade to my freedom. Sensing my nervousness, my puppy raiser gently lifted me up and placed me on the ground. I could run!

And I did! I ran as fast as my little legs could go. I also watched as Decker showed me his skills chasing tennis balls and bringing them back to my puppy raiser.

Wow! Decker is good at that!

My legs suddenly felt very tired. I made my way over to the tiny little human. She seemed busy so I thought I would rest and keep her company.

Out of the corner of my eye, I saw a furry creature racing across the yard.

Another bushy tail!

Just like last time, an encouraging voice called to me. I looked over to see my puppy raiser calling for me. It was still hard to know what to choose. *Should I chase the tail or listen to my human?* The smile from my puppy raiser won out.

Maybe next time…Unless….

Am I not supposed to chase these creatures?

Why might it be important for a guide dog not to chase things?

Rocky is My Name

As the days passed, one thing became consistent—the word "Rocky." When I heard this word, I learned to look up at my puppy raiser. Every time I peeked up at her, she would reply with excitement, "Yes!" and hand me some kibble.

I realized "Rocky" was my name! Now when I heard Rocky, I knew they were talking to me.

Rocky!
Rocky!
Rocky!

I loved hearing my name. It made me feel so important.

I wonder if Rosa and Roxy have learned their names yet?

Learning Commands

My puppy raiser began to practice simple commands to teach me to have good manners. I learned to sit before my meals—*Which is hard!* I had to lay on a mat when everyone was busy—*which is boring!* I also had to be quiet as I stayed in my kennel—*I always fall asleep.*

Around the house, we went 'this way' and 'that way.' My puppy raiser praised me as I trailed after her. I loved following her. Soon, we practiced my commands in different places all around the house.

- ♥ I lay 'down' in the kitchen as I waited for breakfast.
- ♥ I worked on 'back' in the narrow hallway.
- ♥ I practiced 'sit' and 'stay' as my puppy raiser walked around me.

Psst... Decker! Come practice with me.

This was fun!

Every time my puppy raiser gave me a command, I could not move from my position until she gave me the secret word—*Free!*

Every evening, I wandered down the hallway to say goodnight to all three little humans in my new family. The tiny little human liked to hug me tight and murmur, "'Night RockyDecker." She couldn't tell me and my dog brother apart. *I like having a twin name!*

After all the little humans were tucked in, I would sneak into the softest and fluffiest corner of one of the bedrooms for a quick nap.

What is your bedtime routine?

Before she went to bed, my puppy raiser would come get me and carry me to my kennel, tucking me in with a kiss and some kibble.

Chapter 4
Puppy Jacket, Puppy School, and More

The weather became cooler and one day, my puppy raiser said, "Today, Rocky, we're going to practice walking with a leash."

I felt her clip onto my collar. I was curious—*How would this leash walking work?* I looked up to see her hand holding the other end. We were joined together, like a team!

My puppy raiser opened the door, waved her arm and said, "Let's go."

I could smell treats at the other end of her arm, so I followed where she was pointing. The leash stretched tight as I got outside. I sat down and faced her.

> It's important for guide dogs to stop when they enter and exit doors to give the blind person time to pass through safely.

"Yes!" She smiled down at me. She was so excited she almost dropped the treat.

Wow! I did something super important! I thought about what I had done as I nibbled on my reward.

Walking down the driveway, I practiced stopping and starting with my puppy raiser. Each time I followed her lead. When she stopped, I stopped. When she walked, I walked. When she ran, I ran too! *This is fun!*

I was learning that it was important to stay by her side and not pull. She was sending a message that we were working together down through the leash to me. Little did I know how important following this rule would be for my skills.

Is this what it is like to be part of a team?

Puppy Kindergarten

Soon my puppy raiser began taking me to Puppy Kindergarten every week—a fun school just for puppies. In this class, we took turns practicing 'sit' together. We also learned how to be polite when we greeted each other.

I watched the older puppies climb up and down stairs with their own puppy raisers when we had class outside—*I want to be just like them!* I practiced every week. After a while, I could climb up ten steps without stopping!

One time as I tumbled with the other pups, a yippy sound escaped from my mouth.

Whoa, what was that? It surprised even me!

When she heard it, my puppy raiser happily called me to her. "Rocky!" I turned to her—*Ooh—I smell kibble!* I tripped over my feet running to her. She gave me a tasty treat for responding right away to my name.

Little did I realize, my puppy raiser was teaching me that *she* was more important than the barking I had discovered I could do. *Being with her is more fun than anything—more than barking, and even more fun than puppies.*

Guide dogs should not bark as it could cause an issue for their handler.

Putting on My Puppy Jacket

I had learned almost ten commands when my puppy raiser spoke something new. "Get dressed," she said as she coaxed me through an opening in some fabric. It felt a bit scratchy on my back. There was a crackle as the strap was closed under my belly.

"This is to help identify you as you are working, Rocky." Her voice was full of confidence. "It's like your uniform."

I wagged my tail with pride.

I can't wait for others to see my spiffy jacket that shows I am learning to work!

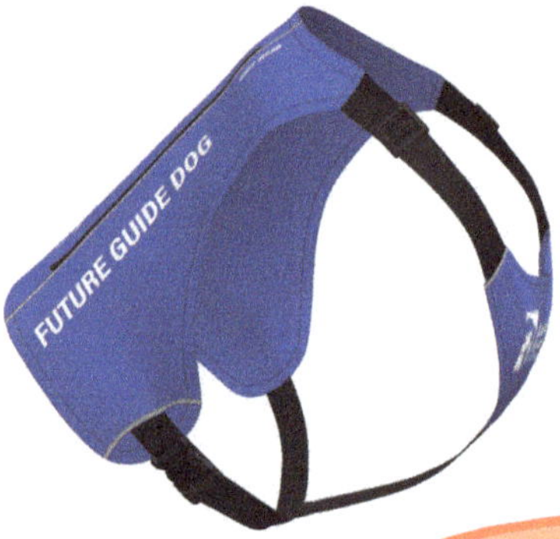

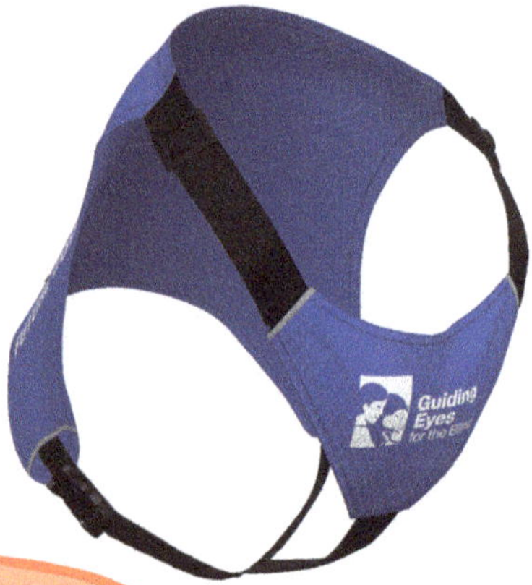

What are some jobs where a person has to wear a special uniform when they are working?

Big Dog Class

Training to be a guide dog meant practicing in many new places. Our puppy class began going on field trips while wearing our official jackets. There were so many distractions, but we were not allowed to stop and sniff anything or say hi to anyone! We always had to stay focused on our puppy raiser.

Guide dogs must always focus on their partner. For this reason, if you ever see a guide dog or guide dog in training, please ask before petting.

"Go place," said my puppy raiser, and I lay on the soft blanket next to her.

"Stand," she spoke as I sat in front of her. I raised myself on all four feet and stood as still as a statue.

"Close," encouraged my puppy raiser as she sat down in a chair.

Hmmm. This was new.

I followed her hand directing me and backed up into a sit, snuggling my tail right against her middle.
Perfect!

Why might a guide dog need to lay really close to their partner?

Every field trip included practicing on different kinds of stairs. We practiced on wooden stairs and metal stairs. When my puppy raiser led me to the bottom of some open-backed stairs, I paused. I could see all the way through to the other side of each step! My stomach dropped.

Oh my… These stairs are the scariest thing I have ever seen.

My puppy raiser said, "Let's go."

I followed her as we climbed up only 2 steps, staying right by her side. Loud noises echoed around us. I could see all kinds of activity through the opening of each step. She encouraged me forward, and we climbed to the top of the stairs together.

Then, she stopped.
Hmmm. Why do I need to stop?

Why do you think learning to stop at the bottom and top of stairs might be important?

I knew to trust my puppy raiser, so I stopped too. She fed me some kibble. I had not actually done anything and yet she had given me a treat. I nibbled away at it and wondered why.

Caring for Me

From time to time, we visited Dr. B. She was my veterinarian. Dr. B would gently poke and prod me to make sure everything was where it was supposed to be. Sometimes I didn't like all the poking. If my puppy raiser saw me tuck my tail a little, she stroked my fur while letting me lick peanut butter off her finger. Special treats like that really helped when I was nervous.

On one of my visits, we gave Dr. B a framed picture of my puppy raiser and me to hang in their office. "Future Guide Dog" was engraved on it for everyone to see.

Each visit after that, I looked at that picture of me and my puppy raiser as I stood on a cold, metal square. They called out a number each time and over time these numbers kept getting higher and higher.

I don't think I can fit on the exam table much longer, Dr. B!

She said I was perfect after every visit. I looked into my puppy raiser's eyes and saw a few tears, but she was smiling. I felt confused. *Is she happy about me getting so big? Or is she sad?*

Every so often my puppy raiser grabbed my care items and sat with me in my favorite spot—the kitchen rug in front of the sink. I could smell that chicken-flavored toothpaste from a mile away—It was spa treatment time!

First, she clipped one toenail—It was hard to keep still but I was rewarded with a yummy swipe of toothpaste.

Then, she brushed my fur a little—I was treated with more teeth being cleaned.

Lastly, she gently wiped my ears—Wow! My whole mouth filled with an explosion of tasty goodness.

I didn't realize it, but she had brushed all my teeth by the time she was done and I loved it!

Chapter 5
Following My Puppy Raiser

Every day with my puppy raiser was filled with activities. When I saw her reaching for my puppy jacket by the door, my heart pumped with excitement.

Yay! Where will we go today? Is it Church Wednesday today? Or Bookstop Thursday?

Some days my puppy raiser went out and I just stayed home in my kennel. But there were times I stayed in my kennel when she was home too. I knew she was home because I could hear the vacuum running or the tiny little human crying.

I lay quietly in the kennel whether she was around or not.

It is important for a guide dog to learn to be calm and settle when needed.

Some days were short bursts of learning. She carried *extra* yummy treats in the pouch she wore and used them to keep my attention as we passed by all sorts of things I might get distracted by.

My puppy raiser makes every day so exciting and fun to learn!

Music, Dinner, and Me

Every Wednesday, my puppy raiser took me and the tiny little human to church for children's choir. Cheerful voices filled a large room as kids giggled and danced to the music. A child whirled past me.

Whoa! Watch out for my paw!

My puppy raiser helped me under the table, away from hopping feet and curious hands. As the children sang and twirled around the room, my ears perked up. I wagged my tail, swinging in time to the beat.
Oh no! I felt a puppy howl trying to wiggle its way out. *I just wanted to sing along!* But I managed to stay quiet. I tucked my paws underneath me while I watched.
After all the kids piled out of the room, my puppy raiser led me out from under the table and down the hall. The floor under my feet went from soft carpeting to slippery tile as we walked closer to the dining hall.
Sniff! Sniff!

Mmm… maybe my puppy raiser will let me taste just a tiny bite?

Sadly, no human food for me. Instead, she played games with me under the table while she ate.
"Touch!" she sang. Under the table, I tapped my nose against her left hand.
"Touch!" she sang again. I lightly touched her right hand up higher.

I loved it when she played with me, but soon she needed her hands to eat, and the games stopped. As I lay down, my eyes felt heavy. Soon, I fell asleep. All around me forks clinked, and people chattered.

I can't wait for my own bowl of kibble waiting for me at home.

A Special School Bookstore

On Thursday mornings we *all* went to a bookstore inside their school called The Bookstop. After eating breakfast, we climbed into our car seats and headed to school.

I waited as they set up a long table, arranged books carefully, and put out chairs for the workers. After my puppy raiser placed a mat on the floor behind her, she told me, "Go place."

I know what that means!

I trotted to my mat, curled up, and settled. Kids lined up and chattered amongst themselves. Next to me, my tiny little human sat in a stroller and nibbled on a snack.

Suddenly, I noticed the tiny little human drop a cheese cracker. I snuck a peek at my puppy raiser—she was busy

counting money. My mouth was watering. I wondered if I could sneak over there to clean it off the floor. *I would be helping keep the floors clean!* The thought was tempting.

But I remembered I needed to remain on my mat. I chose to ignore the tasty treat.

I peeked at my puppy raiser to see if she noticed my good choices, but she was too busy stamping books. I waited patiently until she was free. Then I nudged her and glanced over at the cracker, peeking back at her with my sly eyes. She patted me on the head, "Good boy for not eating that, Rocky."

She noticed!

Kids checked out their final books and then my puppy raiser walked me down the hall to a classroom.

Why are we not going home?

Chairs screeched as kids hurried to their desks, calling out to their friends. My ears flapped from all the excited chatter from the kids when they saw me.

There are so many little humans! And they are so loud!

My puppy raiser started talking to all the kids about me and my future role as a guide dog.

I lay proudly on my mat, my tail swishing left and right. When she stopped talking, the children immediately began asking questions.

"Will he help the blind person drive a car?"

"How does he know when it's safe to cross the street?"

"How does he know where to go to the bathroom?"

Well, I knew the answer to one of those questions, I had a command for it. I was curious about the other ones though.

What else will I learn from my puppy raiser?

I Learn to Settle

As I became more comfortable settling on my mat, my puppy raiser began taking me to places where I needed to settle for longer periods of time—like dentist appointments. She gave me the 'go place' command and I lay on my mat as the kids got their teeth cleaned. This time, grinding and high-pitched noises filled the air. The chairs were huge.

Boy, those dentist tools are loud!

Three kids at the dentist meant there were over fifty teeth to clean. After a while, having nothing to do got a bit, well, boring.

I flipped onto my left side. Then, I flopped to my right. I tried to get my wiggles out without rolling off the mat. My puppy raiser saw me and decided to give me something to do. "Let's do puppy push-ups, Rocky!"

"Down," she said as she pointed. I lay down. She kept going and I kept listening, responding to every command.

"Sit."

"Down."

"Sit."

This was exhausting! But she was giving me something to do that kept me busy, and that short burst of activity was just enough to get my wiggles out.

After we got home, I searched for Decker. Decker listened while I told him all about my adventures.

"You're paw-some," he whispered to me. "Now, rest."

As a grown dog, Rocky will have 42 teeth. How many will you have?

Later that night, dreams of puppy push-ups swirled inside my head as I drifted off to sleep.

Chapter 6
The Real World and Me

My puppy raiser began taking me in my puppy jacket to places with more people and new experiences to practice.

- Grocery Stores—Yummy smells and squeaky carts!
- Traffic Noises—Rumbling engines and beeping crosswalks!
- Sidewalk Adventures—Bumpy grates and people to walk around.

Sometimes she made things happen just to see my reaction—like walking through a giant puddle. *Yuck…*I picked my feet up high the first time, but she had me try it again until I walked all the way through the wet puddle.

"Choo…Choo…" I heard as we walked by a train station.

Whoa! What is that?

My puppy raiser changed from walking slowly to walking fast. I really had to pay attention.

"Good boy, Rocky!" she cheered me on. She was always smiling, making me feel like I could do anything. I learned to ignore all the activity around me and focus only on her.

My heart tugged as I realized how happy she was with my hard work.

Boring Errands

Every Saturday, my puppy raiser took me and the three little humans with her to go shopping. My tail wagged as she put on my coat and we crossed the parking lot, hand in hand, hand in leash, all walking side by side. Once inside, little humans in tow and me by the side of my puppy raiser, we started the journey.

We walked. We stopped. We walked. We stopped. Shopping was honestly, boring.

Suddenly, the tiny little human broke away from our group and squealed "Rocky!" as she tumbled into a fluff ball that looked just like me.

Wait, there's another me?

I stood there and studied it. I felt my ears tuck back. My puppy raiser sensed my discomfort and leaned down next to me.

"Rocky," she said, "Let's check it out!!" But I wasn't sure I wanted to visit this suspicious puppy. It looked like me,

but it didn't smell like a dog. I smelled kibble treats as my puppy raiser's voice encouraged me.

I reminded myself that I trusted her. I inched forward and my tail began to swish. Slowly, I made my way up to the other dog and sniffed. *Nothing!* I sniffed it again and nudged it a little with my nose. *Nothing again!*

Oh, wait! Is this me? I remembered seeing a similar puppy when I was really little.

The tiny little human giggled as my puppy raiser smiled at me. "See, Rocky? There was nothing to be afraid of. I'm so proud of you for visiting this stuffed animal with me." She fed me treats as she said this.

I gazed up at her, knowing I had overcome my fear by trusting her. When she praised me, I knew she believed in me—and I started to believe in myself too!

Traffic and Trails

Soon we took field trips to areas that had lots of traffic and noise. "Heel," my puppy raiser said, and then we began.

I know this one.

Making our way down the sidewalk, I stayed in position next to her as we walked.

Oh no! There is a telephone pole up ahead!

I peeked over at my puppy raiser. Did she see it? Wait, we're going to bump into it!

My tummy tightened in anticipation of what might happen. To my relief, we walked around the telephone pole. And a mailbox. And a lady with a stroller. *Phew! We were safe!*

The smell of grilled chicken wafted into my nose as we walked.

Wait, are we going to brush my teeth here? My mouth watered. *Or get a sample of that delicious-smelling chicken?* Sadly, my puppy raiser did not stop, and we continued walking.

All the people we passed pointed and smiled, admiring me. I stood a little higher and felt more confident. I was proud to be next to my puppy raiser.

Occasionally, I felt my paws curl up as I walked across something cold or uneven, but I kept going.

- Pebbles
- Sewer grates
- Cement
- Dirt paths

Oh my!

I didn't realize it at first, but my puppy raiser was helping me get used to the way the ground could suddenly change. This way when I am guiding someone, surfaces changing would not bother me.

When we came to a street corner, my puppy raiser stopped. Cars were speeding past us as my puppy raiser held tight onto my leash. Suddenly, all the cars stopped.

"Rocky, let's go!"

I stepped down a bit off the curb and we made our way across the street. I glanced over my shoulder and could hardly see where we had started.

Wow, we walked a long way!

Walk and Talks

Every few months a woman named Jane from *Guiding Eyes* came to watch me and all the other puppies in our program. Each one of us showed her what we had been learning.

Jane did the funniest things with us! Sometimes she made all sorts of silly noises. One time she thumped toward me. There was a paper bag covering her head. I tilted my head because I was confused by what she was doing. *Did she think she was scary?*

How silly! Did she think it was Halloween?

But she couldn't fool me! I ran right up to her with my tail wagging and said hello.

It's important for a guide dog to be happy and confident when it sees unusual things.

When Jane left, my puppy raiser gave me an extra good scratch. She whispered in my ear, "Rocky, she says you're going to make an amazing guide dog one day."

I really hoped she was right. I had been working so hard everywhere we went.

So far, I had been inside stores, near traffic, near loud tools at the dentist, and around lots of different people—even tiny little humans.

Every little thing was an opportunity to learn with my puppy raiser.

I wonder where my partner might like to go with me?

Chapter 7
My Family Teachers

Practicing commands out in public was an important part of my training. But sometimes my puppy raiser family just stayed at home and relaxed.

On these days, I loved snuggling in the corner on my favorite pillow while everyone else read quietly or watched TV.

I also learned things when we went to activities as a family. Even though I was not actively practicing commands, these experiences taught me too.

It was like school, but not!

I wore my puppy jacket to these activities too, but it was more about being part of the family and experiencing their life.

Baseball Games

As it got warmer, I started going to baseball games. Decker and I lay on the sidelines while the teams played, and parents cheered. We listened to the thwack of baseballs on bats and whispered to each other, "What are those things called hot dogs that everyone's eating?"

What are some of your favorite activities?

Every so often, my puppy raiser took me for a quick walk around the field. When I saw a shadowy lump on the path ahead of me, my fur hackled a little. I tucked in closer to her. *What is that dark blob?*

"Rocky? Let's check it out!"

She led me with treats and encouragement to this strange object. I sniffed it. I sniffed it again. It just smelled like the outdoors. "See?" she said. "It's just leaves, no need to be scared!"

I looked up at her and wagged my tail. She helped me be so brave. When I got back to Decker, he whispered to me, "What was that about?"

I whispered back, "I defeated the leaf monster!"

Decker nodded his head, understanding. "You, Rocky, are a brave one."

The Bus Stop

Trips in the car allowed me to experience things far away, but just walking out the door allowed me to learn too. When the little humans went to school, we walked to and from the bus stop as the big yellow bus rolled to a squeaky stop right in front of me.

I got used to the ground rumbling as it came near. I watched leaves dance, kids run, and squirrels chase each other. Now I understood to ignore all those furry creatures scurrying by. I stayed at my puppy raiser's side, not paying any attention to those crazy critters.

I also never, ever stopped to use the bathroom while we were walking. I would listen to the command 'get busy' in our yard first, or wait for my puppy raiser to give me the command.

One of the little humans whispered to me about a time his teacher instructed the class to "get busy" on their math lesson. He held his hands over his mouth and secretly giggled. I giggled along with him. What a silly teacher—if she only knew!

> Why do you think it's important for a guide dog not to use the bathroom when it's working?

Decker had been going to the bus stop longer than me. He even waited by the door when it was time to leave. I was so lucky to have him to learn from.

Games Too!

Every so often, my puppy raiser put all the chores aside just to play games with me.

"Rocky, down." I lay on the floor and looked up at her, waiting for what to do next, but she had just disappeared! I sniffed the air.

She's close. I can still smell the grilled cheese on her jeans from lunch.

I had all sorts of wiggles in me. I wanted to burst into a run, but I knew my puppy raiser was counting on me to stay in my down position.

I counted squirrels while I waited. *One…Two….Three…*

"Rocky, come!" Her voice echoed through the halls to me.

Yay! I unfolded my legs from underneath me and set out on my mission to find her. When I did, I got some yummy kibble and a hug.

"You waited a long time, Rocky! Good job!"

Sometimes she tightly held a rope toy and encouraged me to play with her. I gripped the other end with my mouth, and she said "Rocky, out."

I dropped it. Then, she picked it up and we played the game again.

Little did I realize that even when we played, I was learning. She made learning fun!

What games will my partner play with me?

Chapter 8
Fun Time with My Family

I learned in many ways with my puppy raiser family, but I also had fun with them. I sat still as the little humans dressed me up in glorious outfits. I settled quietly in my kennel while the family watched a movie. I watched the kids zipline as Decker dug in the dirt for hidden treasures outside. I tried to help him once, but he whispered, "No, Rocky."

Why do you think guide dogs should not dig holes in their backyard?

As Decker dug his holes, my puppy raiser practiced commands with me.

Treats versus Dirt. Which choice do you think was more fun?

I think I got the better end of the deal.

And I never ever jumped on the couch. Instead, I found somewhere else to rest.

Luckily, my puppy raiser didn't mind me resting on her. She just turned her head to rub my ears. Being close to her, I could feel my heart rate slow down as I settled in for a nap.

I felt my purpose was just being with her, wherever she was.

Trips

There were mornings that we did *not* walk to the bus stop at 7:35 am. In fact, we didn't go to the bus stop at all! I waited for the usual flurry of activity to rush out the door with everyone but there was nothing. I learned these were 'no school' days.

On days like these, we went on extra-cool adventures. Some days, we would take a short trip to the beach. Other times we drove longer to get to the mountains. On these getaways, my puppy raiser tucked away my future guide dog jacket. I needed a bit of encouragement to 'just be a dog,' but that was easy!

At the beach, my paws sunk into the sand as we walked to our tent for shade.

In the mountains, we went for exciting hikes and I doggie paddled through the cool streams.

My puppy raiser rested while she held on to the other end of a long leash.

To help me experience different types of transportation, we even rode the train or the bus on our adventures. One time as we entered a building, I saw the strangest thing.

There's a dog standing at the entrance!

It looked exactly like me, but something was different. I sniffed it and backed up.

That is not a real dog.

The tiny little human was very confused too. We looked so alike!

My puppy raiser told the tiny little human she could pet the dog because it was a statue.

Hmm, I will have to ask Decker what that is when we get home.

Everyone came home from our trips tired. The little humans left to go take their naps. That meant it was just my puppy raiser and me. It was time for cuddles and of course… belly rubs!

What is different between what the statue is wearing versus what Rocky wears as a uniform?

As I fell asleep, I dreamed of all the things that my puppy raiser and I had done together to help prepare me for my future as a guide dog.

Was I ready yet?

Secrets at Home

As quickly as my tail could swish back and forth, 529 days had passed, we had made 712 visits to the bus stop and I had enjoyed more than 1000 bowls of kibble. Many birthday and holiday celebrations came and went with their crunchy paper and leftover boxes to investigate.

I love when one of the boxes I peek into has a gift for me!

Some days were filled with field trips and fun adventures. Some days were spent snoozing during quiet time or just gnawing on puppy toys.

Every day there were, of course, cuddle puddles!

All this time, Decker whispered encouraging reminders to me during our snuggle times.

"Always do the commands the first time you are asked."

"Be happy with your human."

"If you aren't sure what to do, follow the treats."

And then, one day, he whispered… "I think it's time, Rocky."

What does that mean?

How do you feel when someone tells you it's time for a big day at school?

Is It Time?

After all this time, I felt truly connected to my puppy raiser. I tagged along with her everywhere.

- Going to the bathroom? I waited outside the door.
- Vacuuming the family room? I settled on my bed.
- Cooking in the kitchen? Well, I tried to help.

"Oh, silly Rocky!" My puppy raiser giggled. She closed the refrigerator door and sat down with me. "I know you want to help, but pancake-making is for humans."

She led me over to one of the little humans, handing him a book to read.

"Rugby and Rosie," he read, "Just like Rocky and Decker?"

My puppy raiser nodded. "That book will help you understand what you are feeling as Rocky goes into training."

I could sense something different with my family. There was joy, yet sadness. I nestled in closer, trying to provide comfort.

Soon everyone began to scurry around. We were packing for a big trip. I heard the humans say New York. And Guiding Eyes. *That sounded familiar!*

I watched as all our things got packed tight inside the car. The space for my kennel and food was nothing compared to what my puppy raiser family of 5 needed for the trip. Then, it was time to leave but—

Wait! Where's my blanket!?

Decker had shared part of his blanket with me as a going-away present. I wanted it by my side during the next part of my journey. Like she could read my mind, my puppy raiser tucked the blanket into my safe spot and I climbed in. Cuddling it tight, I fell asleep as our journey began.

What will New York be like? What is coming with this next step?

Chapter 9
Professional Training and Me

Our long drive to *Guiding Eyes* took an entire day. There were 3 stops at playlands, about 200 "Old McDonald Had a Farm" tunes, and, of course, many bathroom breaks!

We arrived at the school, and I hopped out of the car. Something smelled oddly familiar. It was a dog smell. It was a family smell. A sister smell—*Roxy was here too!*

I ran over to greet her! Our tails swished back and forth at being together again. I bolted back to my puppy raiser.

Roxy's here too! I showed her by wiggling all over.

She gently patted me on the head and said, "I know, Rocky. You are both back at your first home."

My puppy raiser and the little humans gathered for a final picture.

Then, she handed my leash over to someone new. As someone else walked me back to the testing area, I peeked back at my puppy raiser and family as they called out words of encouragement.

"We're proud of you, Rocky!"

"We love you!"

"You can do this!"

My heart tugged a little as we got farther apart. My tummy flip flopped a little—excited but nervous for what was next.

In for Training Test

As I stood waiting, my feet began to turn cold, and I glanced down. *What is this pile of white fluffy stuff?* I stuffed my nose into it—*Oh my goodness! Whatever this is, it is COLD!*

Before I had time to paw at it, I heard my name.

"Rocky, sit." *I didn't want to sit down in this chilly wet stuff!* I remembered what Decker whispered to me about always doing commands the first time, so I slowly lowered myself into a sit. *BRRRR.*

Suddenly, the next few minutes flew by as things started happening to test my reactions.

- *Swish...sprung the umbrella.* I hopped back, startled, but then walked right up to investigate.
- *Mmm...drifted the smell of a hamburger on the ground.* My mouth watered, but I didn't try to eat it.
- *Rattle...rattle...sounded the can a human was shaking.*

That's loud. I sat, watching, and wondering what the big deal was. I remembered the paper bag lady. *These humans do the silliest things.*

Then, I was led to an office room just like where Dr. B had taken care of me. A man walked in wearing a fancy white doctor coat—*That is not Dr. B!*

His name was Dr. S and he was the veterinarian for *Guiding Eyes*. He peeked inside my ears, rubbed his hands along my belly, listened to my heart, checked my eyes, and looked at my teeth. Finally, he said, "Rocky, you are as healthy as can be!"

I had just passed my health exam and the "In For Training" test. It was the last step I needed before I began my official guide dog training.

I did it!

Rooms and Play Time

All sorts of dogs celebrated my arrival at the kennel we would be living in during professional training. Questions swirled around me and long tails swished in greetings.

"Where are you from?"

"Who is your dog-mom?"

And then, "Psst, over here, you're my roommate!"

I looked up and saw R-O-C-K-Y on the wall next to my kennel space. I walked in and my new roommate and I ran in circles together getting to know each other. Then, we were led to a Community Run for some exercise.

My mouth dropped to the ground when we got there. *Whoa! A gigantic playroom!* There were slides and tunnels and hanging toys, just like when I was little.

What should I do first?

The playroom was filled with dogs also in training. I ran and ran with excitement, but another yellow dog whispered as I scurried past, "Don't forget good manners!"

So, I slowed down a bit and explored the new play area. As I became thirsty, I learned how to use a Lixit, a water bottle for dogs. All I had to do was lick the peanut butter on the dropper of the Lixit and poof! Water dripped right into my mouth!

All the dogs in training became good friends. We ran around, played with toys side by side, and, of course, snuggled together when we got tired.

Then, a trainer was assigned to each of the dogs and the trainer's name written right next to each dog's name. I peeked at the name next to mine, *Jean. What a pretty name!* I tasted it on my tongue. *Jean.*

I can't wait to meet her!

The dogs learn to bond with their puppy raisers and trainers and finally, with their graduate.

Training with Jean

I liked Jean the minute I met her. She snuggled with me in her lap, rubbing my ears as she whispered, "Rocky, I am going to teach you the final steps to help someone live independently."

What does that mean?

Jean gently placed a harness on me. *Ooh, that feels heavy!* I shimmied my shoulders a bit to get the feel of it. It pressed on my back differently than my puppy jacket. I walked back and forth to learn what its weight felt like on me.

I was one of several dogs that Jean worked with. Every day she gathered us together and said, "Okay, pups, it's field trip time!"

The van we rode in was so cool. It was like a double-decker bus! There were two levels of kennels inside, which meant there was a kennel for each of us. Every trip was filled with new things to experience. We each got a turn to work with Jean by ourselves, learning to walk as a team.

I focused hard on what she was teaching me. I moved around people. I ducked under tree branches. I squeezed through tight spots.

There was so much to learn!

- *Back up before turning left.*
- *Slow down before narrow spaces.*
- *Stop at curbs.*

And stairs, again. We practiced on the stairs every single day. By this point, I was a pro!

Suddenly Jean leaned into an object while we were walking. She was going to collide with it! I wanted to bark out, "Watch out, Jean!"

I didn't understand why she leaned into it on purpose. *Why didn't she just avoid it?* I redirected my body to the side of the object as she guided me around it. Jean repeated this over and over.

A guide dog must create enough space around an obstacle so that both the dog and the handler can make it around without bumping into it.

Wait, was I supposed to guide her *around that? Does she not see it?* The next time I saw a large object blocking our path, I walked her around it all on my own.

I get it now!

Days of working together passed quickly and always ended with a hug.

"I'm so proud of you, Rocky!" Jean exclaimed. My tummy did flips of joy.

And you know what? I stood higher and straighter. I was proud of myself too. I could not wait to tell my friends during Community Run time.

Chapter 10
Meeting My Forever Partner

During my final week of training with Jean, students began arriving at the school from all over the country. Chattering and sounds of excitement filled the residential campus at *Guiding Eyes*. Students had arrived to meet their future guide dogs!

Trainers worked with the students doing role reversals. The trainers acted like dogs while the students held the harness. Together, they walked at various paces and tried holding the harness in different ways.

Close your eyes! What would be in your way if you crossed the room?

Looking at their notes, the trainers talked about the students and which dog they would fit best with. They talked about things like "active walker," "needs a good settler in the office," or "has children and needs a dog good with kids."

Questions swirled around all the dogs in the kennel.

"Who do you think is your partner?"

"My last walk around was with someone who smelled like fresh air. I love the outdoors!"

And then, "Psst, Rocky, Jean is coming. It's your turn to find out!"

I heard footsteps coming towards my kennel. I swished my tail with anticipation. Jean peaked in, opened the door, and came into my kennel. She kneeled, and I curled into her lap. She whispered in my ear, *"Connie,"* I heard this word mixed in with some other words.

Who is this Connie person? Is she, my partner?

But I had to wait to find out. I didn't know it then, but I was in for one more surprise!

What surprised you about what Rocky learned in professional training?

A Surprise Visit

As Jean and I walked the busy street during our last week together, I heard children giggling. Their shoes danced on the pavement behind me. Then, a familiar scent wafted into my nose.

Am I imagining this?

Jean stopped. I didn't see any obstacles in our way and waited for her next command. My harness jostled a little and I sensed something different. I recognized the voice that told me to go forward, and I snuck a peek behind me.

My puppy raiser was holding my harness. My heart leaped with excitement!

I can show her all I've learned. Watch me, Mom!

I proudly guided her left and right, around obstacles, safely all the way across the street. Then, the entire family posed for a picture with me.

Later, we spent time together back at the school.

As the day ended, I licked my puppy raiser's face. I wanted to thank her for all she had taught me.

Then, I smelled something else familiar. It was Decker! Even my fur-brother had come to congratulate me!

The visit between Rocky and his puppy raiser family was an exception made at the time they were in the program.

I pranced over to him, and we twirled around each other in a flurry of greetings. I shared with him all the things I had learned. I saved the best news for last.

"My partner's name is Connie." I whispered.

"Rocky," Decker whispered. "You have found your purpose. I am so proud of you!"

As the kids played in the creek, Decker and I settled along the bank. We waited for a chance to splash our paws in the water.

I looked around and realized everyone who had helped me become a guide dog was here with me. Only one more piece of the puzzle was missing.

When will I meet Connie?

Traveling to My New Home

The very next day, there was a flurry of activity as my roommate and several other dogs began meeting their partners. I kept looking outside my kennel, waiting for someone to take me to the meeting place. My heart leaped with anticipation.

Jean came to pick me up and clipped my collar on. I couldn't help but wag my tail with excitement. *This was it! I was finally going to meet my forever partner!*

Instead of heading to the room where my friends were taken, Jean brought me to the van we used for all our field trips. As I hopped into my kennel, questions swirled in my head.

Do I need to learn more?
Why is it only just me?
Oh! Maybe it's a special field trip!

Then, I realized she had brought my blanket from Decker, the one that had traveled with me all the way from my puppy raiser.

I knew where we were going. My heart was racing.
Jean is taking me to meet my partner!

I could not relax during the ride this time. This was it! I hardly noticed the smells of blooming flowers and grills cooking as they wafted in through the open windows.

Then we stopped in front of a large house. My tail didn't stop moving as Jean led me inside. My mouth held tight onto my blanket.

"Rocky, meet Connie. Connie, meet Rocky," Jean said. I carried my blanket with me and sat down next to her.

As Connie rubbed my ears, my whole body filled with warmth. I knew I could trust her just as much as my puppy raiser and Jean. Jean reviewed some basic commands with Connie. She knew all the commands too! Then, Connie sat on the floor, inviting me to her.

Cuddle Puddle!

I couldn't resist this opportunity for a cuddle—all 80 pounds of me!

We spent ten days getting to know each other, and I learned Connie's daily routine. At first, Jean walked behind us to make sure Connie was comfortable. I listened to Connie's instructions of where to turn and guided her around things in our way. When she wanted to cross the street, we worked together to listen and watch for cars.

Our teamwork became as perfect as peanut butter and jelly. She amazed me with how she always knew how many blocks to walk and when to turn. Her confidence in me traveled all the way down the leash. I turned and glanced back at Jean as she watched us with pride.

Then, it was time to say goodbye to my training partner and we watched Jean drive away. My heart tugged a little as I watched her leave, but I already felt a connection with Connie. In my heart, I sensed she needed me. Connie and I were now officially a guide dog team. I thought about all the things I had experienced to get to this point.

- *Fun games that helped me learn commands*
- *Encouraging words, loving pats, and yummy treats*
- *Adventures to many different places*

As we sat together on the porch, Connie invited me up onto her lap.

Finally!

Someone who understood that at 80 pounds I can be a lap dog.

It was something else to love about Connie. She gave me a warm, inviting hug.

My Days

Connie and I spent our days walking to church, the store, the library—all her favorite places. She loved to sneak in a detour to her favorite bakery just for me.

Can you say pumpkin-and-banana-biscuit? Yes, please!

I led her to elevator buttons, guided her through piles of snow on the sidewalk, and settled quietly when she went to dinner with friends.

Connie praised me every time I stopped at the top or bottom of the stairs and when we got to a curb. I could really appreciate all the things people had taught me to help me get ready for my forever partner.

Some days we walked to the nearby park, where I could run free and play with other dogs. I even had playdates with a puppy named Tasha. Tasha became my bestie, and she told me how much happier Connie was with me by her side.

Just like with my puppy raiser, I followed Connie everywhere at home, even when she didn't need me to help her. She was my everything. I was even her travel partner to faraway places!

I loved my new life with Connie. I loved being part of her family. *Sshhh…I even had my own room!*

It is the choice of the graduate to allow their guide on furniture. As a puppy in the program, they are not.

My favorite part of the day was sitting in my very own chair, watching all the goofy squirrels chasing each other outside.

When we were out walking and I saw squirrels running, I never ever chased them. That might cause me to pull Connie down and my job is to always keep Connie safe. She told me every day she was so impressed with me—especially when after multiple trips to the grocery store, I could lead her right up to her favorite ice cream.

Being a guide dog is my purpose. From my time at the Canine Development Center to my puppy raiser, to hours and hours of training, I had been getting ready for this final role. Learning had been hard, but with encouragement, treats, and love, I did it! My life has come full circle and being a guide dog is the best thing I could dream of.

Every day after our activities, every day after our adventures, every day after our trips, Connie always walks into the door with me by her side and says, "Welcome home, Rocky. Welcome home."

"It takes two to tango. Despite what some may think, our guide dogs don't just go it alone. They count on us to provide direction, support, and feedback. We communicate through verbal cues, hand gestures, foot and body positioning, praise, occasional corrections, and physical affection. We're in it together, and we wouldn't have it any other way."
—Pine Tree Guide Dog Users, *Guide Dogs in Action Educational Series*

"Woof, the end!"

Note From the Author

Rocky was with our family for fifteen months, from August 2004 until October 2006. After graduation, Connie came to visit her daughter nearby and we had a celebratory reunion. Rocky greeted us all with tails wags and happy kisses. It was easy to see that he remembered his first family.

Except the baby.

The newest addition to our family had arrived after Rocky graduated. He totally ignored this new tiny little human—no sniffing! No curiosity! Nothing! We all thought this was incredibly funny.

Connie later visited the church where Rocky had spent so much of his time growing up.

As we watched Rocky sniff his way through the halls, it was obvious he remembered his time there—watching children dance, settling during dinners, and sleeping during services. His tail wagged in greeting as he passed familiar people who had watched him in training.

Connie happily answered questions from church members and showed off what Rocky could do. It was exciting for everyone to see Rocky in his harness after watching him learn since he was little.

For a school project, our oldest child had created a mini Rocky, covering it in soft velvet so Connie could feel it. She loved it just as much as my child hoped she would, petting it just like it was her Rocky.

Connie's visit gave us a glimpse into Rocky's new life—a life we'd helped prepare him for.

We couldn't be prouder to see Rocky thriving and helping Connie do the same. With Connie, Rocky had finally become the guide dog he was always meant to be.

Puppy Talk!

Puppy, Puppy, Puppy: Birth through 8 weeks

What is a "litter"? *A litter refers to the number of puppies born at the same time by the same female dog. All the brothers and sisters make up a "litter." Each litter at Guiding Eyes is assigned a letter of the alphabet, starting with A and going to Z. Based on how many litters at the school are born every year, litter names can cycle through the alphabet over 3 times.*

Who are the humans in the first chapter? *The GEB Canine Development Center has an amazing staff that works at the facility caring for the puppies. In addition, there are many volunteers that come in to help and host puppies on their field trips.*

Puppy Raiser Time

What is a Puppy Raiser (PR)? *Puppy raisers are volunteers who take a puppy into their home and provide love, care, training and socialization until it is time for professional harness training.*

Who can be a PR? *You can be a puppy raiser even if you have never owned or trained a dog. Guiding Eyes will support you through the process and teach you what you need to know in order to raise a future guide dog.*

How long is a puppy with their puppy raiser? *A puppy is with his/her puppy raiser anywhere from 12-18 months.*

Training Tools

What is the purpose of the puppy jacket? *When puppies wear their jacket, it tells those around them that they are working. The jacket has special words on it that say 'Future Guide Dog' and 'Guiding Eyes for the Blind'.*

Why is a kennel used? *If a puppy is not able to be supervised, they relax in the kennel so they cannot get into mischief! The kennel becomes a puppy's special retreat, and they find comfort being in it.*

What is a harness? *The harness allows the handler to feel the dog's movements and works as a special tool that allows the dog and blind partner to have a special connection, providing the team instant safety and communication.*

Going Back to School

What is an IFT test? *A guide dog puppy going In For Training is a very important step. The IFT is a special test, almost like an end-of-grade test. Each pup has a series of tests to evaluate their response to stressful situations, their knowledge of commands and also their house manners.*

What is a guide dog graduation? *A match between a dog and their handler is a celebration! There are formal graduation ceremonies on campus for all students, whether it's their first, second or tenth guide dog. Puppy Raisers are invited to the IFT as well as the graduation. They are also invited to visit with the dog prior to completing a home training, which is how Rocky graduated.*

How does a guide dog know how to cross the street? *The dog's handler learns to judge the movement of traffic by following sounds. Dogs don't see colors the same way we do. They definitely can't read traffic lights! When the handler decides that it is safe to cross, he or she will give the dog the command, 'forward,' in order to move out into the street. Guide dogs are also taught 'intelligent disobedience.' If there is an obstruction in the street or an oncoming vehicle that poses a danger, the dog will choose not to listen to the 'forward' command. In this way, the guide dog keeps his handler safe.*

Guide Dogs with the Handler

What kind of toys and games can a guide dog play with when not working? *While a guide dog is taught to not play fetch or dig holes, it still runs and frolics like a regular dog! There are approved toys for guide dogs to play with as well as games to play–just like Rocky did with his puppy raiser.*

How do graduates know when dogs need to go to the bathroom and/or know how to pick it up? *Guide dogs are taught to only use the bathroom on command. When the handler gives the command, they check the dog's back. If it's diagonal, the dog is peeing. If the back is hunched, the dog is pooping! The handler puts their foot near the dog's back leg so that once the dog is done, they can search the area for easy clean up.*

What should I do when I see a working guide dog team? *First off, don't be afraid to talk to a blind person. People always like to know you admire their dog. If you wish to assist a person with a guide dog, first ask "May I help* you?" If they say yes, then offer your left elbow. Do not reach for the guide dog, the leash or harness, or the person's arm. Doing so may place them in danger.

Can I pet a guide dog in harness? *Guide dogs should not be petted or disturbed while working in harness - they have a very important job to do! They are the eyes of their partner and need to stay focused. The same is true of any dog that you may encounter. You should never pet a dog without asking permission first.*

And finally…

How long does it take for the dog to be fully guiding? *It can take anywhere from 18-24 months before a dog graduates as part of a guide dog team.*

What happens to dogs that do not make it through the program? *Dogs that don't meet the criteria for guide work can become detection dogs, search and rescue dogs, therapy dogs, or cherished family pets. Regardless of the career paths our dogs choose, puppy raisers and GEB are immensely proud of each one of them.*

What can I do to help with a puppy like Rocky? *You can do a lot of things! You can become a puppy raiser. You can volunteer with a puppy raiser group near you. You can even be a puppy sitter for a day. You can show your knowledge about guide dogs or other service dogs by remembering not to pet a working dog.*

And of course you can share Rocky's story with your friends!

Thank you for adding *Rocky, Life as a Guide Dog Puppy* to your library. If you and your child enjoyed this story, please consider posting a thoughtful review on Amazon, Goodreads or other favorite book site. Your kindness will make a difference for others considering this book.

Proceeds from *Rocky, Life as a Guide Dog Puppy* are donated to Guiding Eyes for the Blind® to assist in providing training for present and future guide dogs.

Did I catch your attention?

Guiding Eyes for the Blind® provides dogs that can be matched with their partner in a variety of ways. Let me tell you about the different options for placement.

- On Campus/Residentail Training
- Home Training 
- Specialized Training
- Running Guide Programs

Author recommendation
Read about a pup like Rocky!
Rugby and Rosie
By Nan Rossiter

Rugby and Rosie is a children's story about a young boy and his best friend, Rugby, a chocolate Lab. When Rosie, a future guide dog puppy, comes to join the family, Rugby isn't quite sure about her. He ignores the pup who barks at him, climbs over him, and won't leave him alone, until one day he has a change of heart. The inseparable threesome launch into the blissful days of summer, with the boy knowing that their companionship and adventures together are not going to last. Come autumn, Rosie will be going to school to finish her training to be a guide dog.

I purchased *Rugby and Rosie* for our oldest child before we brought Rocky into training at Guiding Eyes for the Blind–the same school Rosie went to. I will never forget him walking to me after reading the book, tears in his eyes. The story spoke to his heart. The words perfectly described the emotions of being a puppy raiser. As I continued to raise more puppies for Guiding Eyes, I brought the book with me to schools. It helped me talk to kids about the important role of guide dogs. Likewise, when I worked as a therapy dog team, the book was one of my reading tools. Rosie looked just like my therapy dog, Brisco!

I recommended *Rugby and Rosie* to other puppy raisers in my area to help with their transition of turning in a dog for training. The illustrations are beautiful and the story is a perfect testament to the love and dedication a puppy raiser has in giving the gift of their time to prepare a dog for their future.

Consider purchasing a copy for yourself, or donate a copy to your local school or library!

Electra and Rhythm highly recommend *Rugby and Rosie* as well. Electra is currently a working guide dog, and Rhythm is a therapy dog extraordinaire. They were both raised by Janet Mills who owns Rhythm & Co. Books, where Rhythm continues to review books on a regular basis.

Acknowledgements

Guiding Eyes for the Blind® provides guide dogs to people with vision loss. They are passionate about connecting exceptional dogs with individuals for greater independence.

Rocky is one of thousands of graduated service dogs since the founding of Guiding Eyes in 1954. Guiding Eyes has managed to thrive on goodness, even in the most difficult of times. They rely on the goodness of their loyal base of generous supporters, passionate staff and dedicated volunteers to come together to meet the growing needs of their diverse community of people with vision loss. Through this unwavering support and dedication, Guiding Eyes has graduated more than 10,000 guide dog teams. They believe in the powerful, meaningful change that their beautiful dogs bring to the lives of people facing the daily challenges that blindness and vision loss present.

Guiding Eyes is a 501(c)(3) nonprofit organization with all services provided completely free of charge.

The journey from playful pup to professional Guiding Eyes dog takes up to three years and can cost up to $50,000 annually. As a 501(c)(3) nonprofit organization, they provide all services completely free of charge to people who are blind or experiencing vision loss. At Guiding Eyes, they rely upon the contributions of their generous donors to fulfill their mission.

With nearly 150 employees, Guiding Eyes operates out of their 10-acre Headquarters and Training Center in Yorktown Heights, NY, and their Canine Development Center in Patterson, NY, as well as their field-training center in White Plains, NY. Their puppy raising regions stretch from Maine to North Carolina and west to Colorado.

More than 1,700 volunteers are a vital part of the Guiding Eyes community. They participate in everything from raising, training, and socializing potential guide dogs to supporting their day-to-day operations. To learn more about supporting our mission, please visit:

https://www.guidingeyes.org/

*Proceeds from *Rocky, Life as a Guide Dog Puppy* are donated to Guiding Eyes for the Blind® to assist in providing training for present and future guide dogs.

Meet the Author

Margot with future service dog, Barley, Feb. 2022

Margot has trained with over 10 dogs during the last 25 years. She has served as a puppy raiser for ten service dogs and worked with her therapy dog, Brisco, for ten. She firmly believes that all dogs have a purpose, and that belief has propelled her to volunteer in multiple dog placement programs that service communities.

Rocky, Life as a Guide Dog Puppy is her third children's story in the series Tails Of Dogs Who Help. *Ely, Life As A Service Dog Puppy*, is her second children's story in the series and tells of Ely's journey prior to finding his forever partner. The first book in the series, *Brisco, Life As A Therapy Dog*, tells the story of Brisco's work in the community helping others.

In telling the stories of the many dogs she has raised, Margot is excited to teach the message of what our dogs can do for us–whether it be through therapy or through service. Her hope is these books will be a fun way to educate kids about how these dogs become who they are meant to be by telling it through the eyes of the dog.

Margot Bennett is based in North Carolina and married with four children. When she's not working with dogs, helping with homework, or volunteering at schools, you can find her hiking, swimming, or hiding out in her nook working on scrapbooking, playing the drums and dreaming of when her next service dog puppy will arrive.

She is excited to be working on her fourth book in the series. *Barley, Life as a Facility Dog Puppy* will be available in 2024!

Want to learn more?

Visit Margot's website: dogswhohelp.com

Follow all the Bennett dogs on Instagram:
    @tailsofdogswhohelp
and on Facebook:
    facebook.com/Tails-Of-Dogs-Who-Help

Margot's books available on Amazon

Comparison	Service Dogs	Therapy Dogs	Emotional Support Dogs
ADA Covered: Rights to bring animal into public establishments.	✓	X	X
Needs to tolerate a wide variety of experiences enviroments & people.	✓	✓	X
May live with their disabled owners, even if "No Pets" policy in place.	✓	X	✓
Primary function is to provide emotional support, through companionship.	X	X	✓
Specifically trained to assist just one person.	✓	X	X
Provide emotional support and comfort to many people.	X	✓	X

Coming Soon!

The next book in the series

Tails Of Dogs Who Help
Book 4

Barley, Life as a Facility Dog Puppy

Meet Barley, a handsome yellow Lab/Golden Cross who tells the story of his journey becoming a Capitol-Facility Dog. Follow his life from being born into the B litter, to working with a puppy raiser and finally graduating into professional training, where he finds the perfect handler to work with as a Facility Dog.

www.ingramcontent.com/pod-product-compliance
Lightning Source LLC
Chambersburg PA
CBHW040732220426
43209CB00087B/1607